LIVING FIRST

WAKEY, WAKEY!

Alphabet of Living

(the way your nature intends)

www.livingfirst.co.uk

CONTENTS

Introduction

Ah! There you are,

Here's something different to keep the old grey cells, the new, vibrant and all those in between ticking over alive and living.

'Life is much less tangible than we think and yet,

everything we are affects

everything we are and

everything life is.

It is, therefore, extraordinarily important that

we are all we can be – inside, out and throughout.'

Living First and its therapies are all about living well – healthy, happy, shiny, thrivy, alive and living - inside, out, throughout and, most importantly – for the whole of your life.

Here's how !

Z to A of Living to help you on your way

Enjoy!

Z is for...

Zen...

Beyond all ken,
yet enwrapped, immersed,
submerged and interspersed within it.
It is life, it is pure, it is beauty,
it is grace, it is light, it is alive, it is joy
Zen is whole
Zen is one
Zen is being at one in an wholistic whole
Zen is one wholly in the zone.

I love everything Japanese. Actually, that's a big statement, too big really – I should say, I love some things Japanese.

I love Reiki, their art, their joy, their forests, their grace, their simplicity, their attention to detail, their expertise and subtlety of passion for getting things just so.

"it

is

the

quiet

respect

for

everything

and

nothing

–

it

is

Zen"

From Samurai warriorship, sashimi, carpentry, teapot making, traditional tatami flooring on which to sleep – even the stony pillows, their ryokans with community bathing and showering, minimalism and phenomenal use of space.

'It is the quiet respect for everything and nothing

- it is zen.'

How's your Zen?

You too were born to shine and thrive...

... how's your art of living your life?

Is your life open to that of master craftspeople...?

They're easy to spot - they show a level of mastery, precision, beauty, artistry and grace – oneness. This level of human existence is alive in all humans – we each have moments of vital connection to that experience of oneness; when we are in the zone.

If your world doesn't have such craftspeople to move and inspire you, invite them in.

Here's how:

Open your senses, loosening them, breathing life in, out and all around allowing any tensions to disperse in their own sweet way.

Invite in 'being whole', being one, being one of the whole.

When it hits home, appreciate and enjoy the sensations, allowing them to spread throughout, relaxing, calming, softening, loosening and opening some more; a gentle smile forming.

Live, breathe and be it – being 'at one'.

Then when you do find yourself smiling, radiating throughout, you will know - your own zen-like qualities are alive and living in all you are and all you do... x

Y is for...

You

Gosh where do we start – what makes
you, You?

You are unique.

Every single atom of your being is alive with everything you are – everything that makes you you – your you-ness...

Your... soul, spirit, body, mind, emotionality, motionality, vibe, tribe, senses, nature

... still with me...? There's more...

Your... instincts, intuitions, pleasures, pains, talents, gifts, abilities, skills, strengths, vulnerabilities...

Your experiences to date...

Your moment right now...

Your future...

Everything in the whole wide world that floats your boat… and everything that makes it sink.

Moment by moment, day by day, circumstance by circumstance,

Your life is totally unique to you.

You, your history, your future, your life right now, is very special indeed.

Phew!

As well as all that…

There are some things, many things we all share: the Universe, our planet, the 'other-worldly', our humanness, our life.

'Be yourself, live your life and enjoy yourself on the way'

were words that bubbled up for me the other week and made me realise I somehow needed permission to enjoy being me!

This is understandable.

We all live through challenges way before we're equipped to do so well. This can and does take its toll.

The best we can do is connect freely with all that endures no matter what – inside and out, opening ourselves to everything that nourishes whilst letting go of everything we became to survive.

You have all the permission in the world to enjoy being all you are and all you are to be, and just to make doubly sure…

I hereby give you all the permission you will ever need…

Be You x

Here's how:

Taking time out is super important anyway – taking time out - WHEN YOU DON'T NEED TO is a great way to start getting your whole act together.

"whatever

we are

on the

inside,

we are

in

the

outside

world"

X is for...

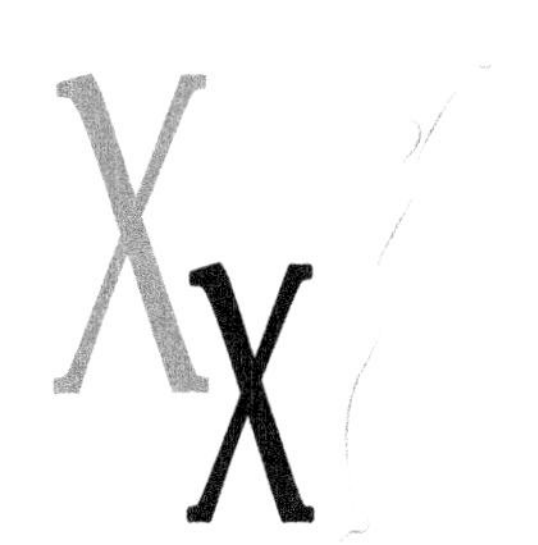

Xenophobia

Before we begin, I just need to point out
that being fearful of others, xenophobia is different to living in fear of someone. If you are living in fear of someone, please get immediate help.

Humanness is one of our strongest connections - it is also the strongest force for keeping us apart.

The root of the word xenophobia is from the Greek, xenos, meaning stranger and phobos, meaning fear.

Xenophobia is fear of strangers… and as we all know, there's nowt as strange as folks... !

... and we are each completely unique individuals. So when you think about it, unless we get that spark of connection from the get-go, it's impossible to feel comfortable with other people, until such time we get to know each other a little.

The problem with xenophobia is that we never reach that point of getting to know the other. Instead we shut ourselves off and shut 'them' out.

"All relationship building forms threads of interconnectivity around our innate human connection."

Threads such as: shared meaning, language, humour, activities and behaviours. Whilst this process builds relationships between people, they can also cloud our innate connectivity - humanness, disconnecting us from all who don't possess those same threads.

Awareness of self and others is an important factor of life. Tangled it becomes too conscious making us too self-conscious and other-conscious. Untangled it allows us to be an active participant throughout our life with other people.

So, whenever we find ourselves out of our comfort zone, with people who are different to ourselves, it's understandable we do so from a position of discomfort that manifests in a vast array of forms. No matter what, any form of discomfort sends out vibes. We're stressed, we send out stress vibes that resonate throughout.... Like ripples on a pond.

Any discomfort, and we revert to self-defence; a self-protective barrier, until such time mutually interactive behaviours are established (or not). Throughout this process of establishing living arrangements between people, some behaviours will present as xenophobic. However, as long as there is some level of mutuality alive and living in both, conscious or otherwise, there will be some form of mutual progression.

Xenophobia becomes problematic when there is zero mutuality and that gapping is filled with either bad feelings or trauma.

When filled with dark energy, xenophobic behaviours are seen to be rude, ignorant, simultaneously social and anti-social or being distant when around certain others. Some of these behaviours are totally unconscious and purely habitual, others are more transient; mere temporal experiences connected with adaptation to life's changes.

Fear, on the other hand, happens when confrontation with a stranger is marked with a shift out of our comfort zone with which we can't cope and fear takes over. All of which is either the mark of past trauma or inexperience. Either way it's important that the experience of fear doesn't get stuck.

No-one need live in fear. However, our fight/flight can become stuck, become ingrained and switching on in seemingly non-threatening situations, closing down our wider senses. As such, we act threatened and others respond accordingly.

Just to confuse, we could just be having an off day.

The point is, we are all human, I am human, you are human and so too is everyone else… imperfect ones at that.

No matter what, we are better for ourselves and everyone else without these patterns that cut us off from others.

Here's how:

You are human... and so too is everyone else.

Allow the words to light your spark of humanness inside. Take time out, allowing it to spread in its own good time. Begin to enjoy the pleasure of being human and being around others who allow you to be more so – more you.

Even though life is extraordinarily complicated and we don't always act it, you are human and so too are the rest of us.

You don't have to be friends or friendly with everyone - just be yourself: safely, securely, comfortably, alive and living your life to the full - shining and thriving… with a willingness to hold a mirror up to yourself… honestly.

Enjoy being yourself, your humanness.

Begin to enjoy the sometimes inconvenient truths that arise about yourself and others... humour eases healing and progressive transformation.

Begin to like yourself,

Begin to love yourself inside, out and throughout.

Open yourself to being freely open with all those who enjoy, like and love you and who you enjoy, like and love.

Be freely open with those who enjoy, like and love the things you do and freely open with those who do what you enjoy, like and love.

You are human, you are unique... and so too is everyone else.

As difficult as being human is, it is better than okay – it is pretty amazing.

Yep, we are pretty amazing

"everything

we are

affects

everything

life is

everything

life is

affects

everything

we are"

W is for...

Want

'Getting what you want isn't all it's cracked up to be'

A phrase I've heard many times in my life... I just want to say... it can be, as long as it is an wholistic want. That is as and when our whole self is on board with it.

So where does a non-wholistic want come from?

It's a shortcut - a direct link from the guts to the mouth… a baby's 'Mwah!' becomes 'I want!'

Yes, super, fine in a baby expressing itself in that way – top marks. However, not so attractive in an adult – when it turns into demands that insist on being satisfied.

The Mwah! Has its place. It's a natural, wholistic reaction and as such must be respected, appreciated, heard and responded to. However, as we grow we can fall prey to getting our way this way... as well as letting others get their way too.

To progress beyond our own Mwah! requires that we open ourselves to hearing our own – with an open honesty.

A story:'

When my husband and I began to make this last move, we had no idea it was happening. Yes, apparently Devon and the sea had been on the cards for some time, but they were so deeply buried in our subconscious we had no clue – nobody did. So it was all a bit of a shock when one thing led to another and we found ourselves travelling around this way, reaching Dartmouth and getting an immediate connection to it. Quite disconcerting in many ways. It was totally foreign and yet… Our second visit confirmed it – for me at least – I didn't want to leave.

My reaction to this unconscious want being satisfied was bizarrely foreign. You see I wasn't brought up to have my wants satisfied – to have 'my way'. I was brought up to be part of a family who pulled their weight and resources to make our going easier all round. Grateful – for the food on our table, the clothes on our back and the roof over our heads. When I was warm, had shelter and food readily-ish available, I was satisfied – what more could I want! So yes, this level of satisfaction was totally alien and yet, something pleasant I could not ignore – I felt at home and I wanted to settle here.

One thing led to another and within a year we had moved. During which time many things appeared on our wish/want list. Little did we know the essence of which was our souls crying out to be at home, to be settled (and not), doing all the things that make us come alive.'

So, yes, let your wants, wishes, desires, fantasies, dreams and imaginings have 'their airing', express themselves, letting them go as freely as you like, off into the ether.

When you are being true to yourself, the Universe, Nature, Your Nature, you are aligned with everything… there will be work involved on your part to make things happen – work that, in the long run will be its own reward.

No matter what, when those wants, wishes etc. ring true, they will bear the sweetest fruit.

"wishes that are true bear the sweetest fruit"

Here's how:

Open to healing your bruises, knocks and scrapes,

Open to being free to be your all,

Open to being the person you like, love, enjoy,

Open to feeling really, really good about being and doing your all,

Open to being your sparkle,

Open to being with sparkles of light that help guide your way, and yes,

Open to being honest, at least with yourself.

V is for…

Vibe

Being your vibe isn't something to find,
learn or work out – it's something that just is.

Your vibe is you being you – the real you – the you who knows you are being yourself – inside, out and throughout.

Somethings about your vibe…

It has to be pleasant – there's a rightness about it, a clear brightness that hits all the right spots just so – nourishing your soul.

Your vibe changes with age, situations and circumstances – as you transform so too does your vibe. It's like your wholeness is a cocktail of energies – a vortex of living gloop that is undeniably connected to, and affected by the whole of everything else. Yet also a totally unique recipe, which in turn has its effects on everything else.

There are things that resonate, things that don't and a whole heap of other stuff in between.

Some things float away, others rankle, then there are those that just soak all the way through. Just be aware there's always developing, progressing and growing to do.

Your vibe is unique to you and it's important to attune to, resonate with and be drawn to everything that energises – allowing you to shine and thrive.

Here's how:

If you haven't already done so, open yourself to abundance, part of which is you being your vibe.

Freeing yourself, let go of everything and anything that might be stopping it from happening.

Then, when things do 'hit the spot' – enjoy, allowing the sensations to spread throughout...

Little by little, and as gently as you like begin to allow yourself to discern, quite organically, between those that nourish and those that drain.

Welcoming in more of the former and letting go the latter, letting them go on their way.

U is for...

Universe

Being universal is a bit weird, because we
are just that – Universal... and there's no getting your head around it.

Rather, accept it, being at peace with everything you are.

Yes, you are universal… and as we've seen in 'Y', so much more. Being universal affects all of that.

'In the zone' or 'having a moment', are the closest I can get to describe experiencing being universal.

Have you ever experienced it? It's like there are no edges, no friction, no conflict… green lights all the way – inside, out, throughout - we are the Universe, living and breathing universality; we are universal.

When we're not 'in the zone' we still remain universal, just not 'at one' with it and to be so would be an impossibility. We have to live, right!

It's like those moments of clarity and smooth, clear running, when there's no stopping us, are snapshots of amazingness that tell us there's a whole heap of life beyond ourselves... that is also ourselves.

The tricky bit is the fact that all life is affected by every single effect of every single universal happening.

It's all a bit wow!

The whole of life is 'the Universe', spawned of itself into a form; an existence. Living, that is, the act of being alive and living is really quite beautiful, some might say, heavenly. However, we all know don't we that living does also have its edges and these can at times be a living hell. Saying that, clearing our universal connections and becoming more centred and grounded makes living it all a whole lot easier.

There is no 'how to' to this one – it just happens.... and, if you're anything like me, the 'oh my goodness – how do I even begin to live now!' happens soon afterwards.

It's euphoric, mind-blowingly so and the ultimate pleasure of infinite connectivity.

In amongst all of that is you living your life (for real!), dreaming your dreams, living your life and making our future.

So yes, a bit of a tricky beast when that euphoric moment hits home – and one that's tricky to live well (I certainly didn't! And yes, that is a whole other story for another time!)

Here's how:

Just be, soak it all in, around and throughout. Panic not (although this might be difficult – just let that be too), allowing yourself to immerse in it all, be embraced by it wholistically, embracing it all, calming, relaxing, loosening and melting, clearing and renewing your connections to your wholistic self, life and everything.

Yes, it is the ultimate in letting go.

Being and breathing as softly, gently as you like (or can), welcoming in this new phenomenal phenomenon into the whole of you, everything that endures no matter what, your essence, past, presence, potential and future.

Closing your eyes and, if possible drifting off into a gentle slumber.

Yes, be with

"sometimes

the best

and

sometimes

the worst

things

happen

for

no

reason"

T is for...

TT

Transformation

Had to be didn't it!

We morph, we change, we live, experiencing our lives and adapting; every moment of every day, we are transforming.

Some things suit, some do not, others are neither here nor there. Others bring out the best in us, others the worst. The important thing is what we become.

When living the things that suit, we're given respite to be ourselves, living a life that suits us wholistically - at that point in time. If our lives were being filmed and those frames frozen in time, they might be witnessed as someone *just* being themselves, blending in well, natural and playing their part to the full in the whole with ease. Quite bizarre really, when in reality we are living at an optimum. I say, 'an' optimum, as, of course, there are many variations.

That said, in amongst all the noise and hullabaloo of the rest of life happening, these momentary threads of peace, tranquillity, serenity, wholeness, fullness and oneness are predominantly overlooked – yes, even by ourselves.

These moments are our most precious.

Living with people who are shining and thriving is precious… from which we all benefit. Yes, we all benefit from you being just so… and so, the more you are 'just so', the better life is all round.

Here's how:

Next time you are 'just so', take another moment or few out, enjoying the sensations the experience brings, breathing them all around and throughout.

Loosening, untangling, freeing yourself of unnecessary ties.

Opening yourself to abundance

Connecting with, engaging, experiencing and benefitting from the mere act of just being with new, renewing living circularities.

Transformation Turbulences will happen.

Let it be, letting go, sending all and any toxicity on its way...

"your

soul

knows

where

to go

for

nourishing

growth"

S is for...

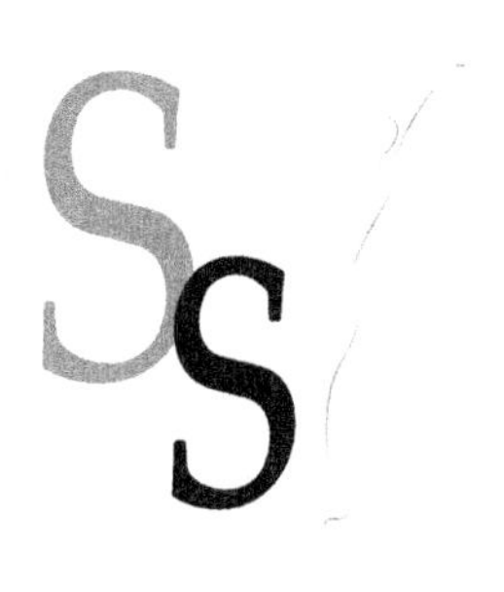

Social, Sociability, Society

There's nothing like a good battle, a bit of conflict to realise one of our most precious fundamentals in life - the importance we humans are to each other. And Covid-19 provided just such a battle to bring being social, our sociability and society to the forefront of everybody's minds, bodies, presence and futures.

It's a tricky one though isn't it... here's why:

To be social we have to connect to another in some way, and, because no two people can possibly be compatible all the time, we also develop ways of living with others whilst side-stepping and compensating for those many, many differences.

Now, when you begin to consider just how many levels there are on which to connect, disconnect and side-step, we begin to realise not only just how tricky being social is, let alone sociability and society, but also the phenomenality of when we do connect and synergy flows.

"humans

are

such

complex

beings

that

any

form of

synergy

is a

minor

miracle"

Here are the many levels of existence on which we connect etc.:

Universality, Nature, spirituality, our individual nature, behaviours, activities then there's: the physiological, biological, familial, vibrational, environmental, linguistics, presence, identity, influence and technological.

All of which affect our, spiritual, emotional, rational, intellectual, spatial, cultural, political, economic, personal preferences and personal prejudices.

Phew! That's a lot of levels on which to engage others – yet we do!

On top of which, we are all continually affecting change in the whole of everything, as well as being affected by everything else every single moment of every single day.

How amazing are we!

Yes, I know, we have much work to do to improve things…

The problem is that we are sensitive creatures and when our sociability is knocked off course, our most tender and vulnerable senses that together provide our sense of belonging, take the knock, becoming bruised, sometimes traumatised.

Whilst everything is affected, our softer side suffers most – our emotions, playfulness, humour, joy, character, kindness, compassion, generosity etc.. All of which has an ongoing effect on hope, faith, trust and charity – free, full living space inside, out and throughout.

Human sensitivity should not be a problem.

In fact, human sensitivity should be quite the opposite – a cause for celebration!

Human sensitivity is in fact the cornerstone of what makes us beautiful creatures on this amazing planet of ours.

"Human sensitivity needs to be nurtured to live as

freely and fully as possible,

as this is what makes us human,

and allows us to live our lives to the full."

Such is life just now.

That's it guys, to reclaim all that good stuff for ourselves we have to take our chances – let go all else and go for it – for shining and thriving!

Fundamental to that happening is our innate ability to nurture and opening ourselves to life progressing self-nurture.

Our softer parts are our most precious elements, bringing our most gentle, most authentic selves to the fore with a warmth of energy, we can do nought else but smile. It's like all our bits are being massaged in the gentlest possible way, filling with our gorgeousness, bringing to life our emotional beingness and allowing it to live and breathe through us.

Here's how:

Cut yourself some slack – and everyone else for that matter...

Open yourself to giving yourself a break whilst being your best for yourself, everyone and everything else: resting, recovering, healing, replenishing, renewing, restoring, re-energising, re-enlivening in whichever shape or form suits you best – at your own best time and pace... being aware, of course that your whole knows best...

your soul knows...

Get out and about in nature, let your body breathe fresh air, cleansing the parts other stuff just can't reach - and begin to enjoy doing so.

Open yourself to being yourself, worldly and wholly aware, whilst beginning to live like there's no one watching – and enjoying doing so.

Enjoy clearing debris, generating more living space inside, out and throughout.

Oh my goodness, beginning to feel the joy of breathing - being alive and living!

Fill your life up to overflowing with all the people and all the stuff that allows you to be your best version possible: you being you, 'knowing' you are being yourself.

Become saturated in yourself, all your gorgeousness.

Immerse yourself in the whole of life, all its gorgeousness to emerge anew – refreshed, renewed.

R is for…

Reiki

Reiki signifies a specific connection and relationship with universal energy that allows us to let go for a while, reconnect and re-engage our qualian beingness – those subtle nuances that make you you on a Universal level.

[Other such untangling practices are available.] ;-)

Words to the wise: phenomena such as Reiki often fall prey to the vagaries of our rational minds. The best way for it to be approached is as openly, as loosely calm and relaxed as you possibly can.

Whenever synergy happens between the person channelling and recipient, Reiki is: relaxing, calming, nourishing, untangling, releasing, renewing, re-energising, replenishing, re-engaging and re-enlivening – with the potential to be life-changing.

There are, of course many ways by which we engage, cleanse and heal universal connectivity, thereby renewing and re-enlivening ourselves, of which Reiki is one.

For me, the thing we call Reiki was just part and parcel of who and what I was and had always been from a very young age. It was just something I lived and breathed. I only connected with it on a professional level when one morning I awoke with the word, Reiki on my mind with a will to find out more about it. It was quite bizarre to realise that something that came quite naturally to me was being practiced professionally.

To me, Reiki is an art form and part and parcel of my art of living.

Such phenomena become recognised through the passage of time. One person's actions beneficially affect the life experience of another. It is experienced, witnessed and, as and when the culture is open to the practices, it's left to be. From there it becomes whatever it is to the individuals concerned.

Reiki allows me to practice and experience the ultimate in universal synergy – temporary life enhancing connections on a purely energetic level for relaxing, calming, clearing and healing. As such it re-enlivens the senses, instincts, intuitions – the individual's Nature.

I love it, and to be able to practice it is both a blessing and a privilege.

When it works, Reiki is a truly beautiful experience.

Sometimes it happens, other times it doesn't. However, it is important to be with any draw you might have to give it a go…

… when free to do so, the soul knows where to go for nourishing growth,

… and whilst sometimes we don't like where it's taking us,

… other times, yes, it's good to go… to be with the flow.

Here's how:

It's all about relationships, your circularities with the whole of the rest of life – and yes, as you are connected to the whole of life, you will already have your own circularities with the universal aspects of life – inside, out, throughout and beyond.

Just allow those words to sink in and flow around to their own accord.

You are a Universal being and it matters not a jot how that plays out in life – as long as it is alive and living through you as free-flowing as is possible.

Being well-hydrated helps clear our debris no end.

Relaxing, calming, loosening, opening up and breathing as freely as free can be. The connection and relationship is there… enjoy.

Let your whole self be your guide…

Q is for...

Quantum

Quantum is the minimum amount of energy required for an interaction. That is the absolute minimum required to have an effect. And that is teeny, so very teeny, it's beyond our comprehension for anything so teeny to have an effect on anything else, and yet there it is – something so teeny yet interacts and has effect.

This phenomenon is important as it marks a ground zero in life, living, being and being alive and living. It also shows us the extent to which we are being affected, bombarded if you like every moment of every day by things beyond ourselves. Oh yes, and the affect our actions have on everything else.

Once you begin to open yourself to realise this level of effect on us all, cutting ourselves a little more slack becomes a whole lot easier – allowing us to appreciate the little things of life: being alive, living and everything that nourishes, all that little bit more.

Here's how:

Get yourself comfortable, well-hydrated, safe and sound.

Let your body breathe.

Open your senses to the whole of life around you – inside and out.

Feeling the sensations of where your body meets the outside world, letting the tiniest of interactions happen, through your senses, relaxing as you go.

Move, stretch, be alive with the flow, loosening and letting any debris go.

Deepen your breaths, enjoying the sensations of being alive and enlivening everything you are – allowing a soft smile to form of its own accord.

As gently as you like – as and when,

Let your brain melt, flowing freely throughout.

Filling your lungs to the full, reaching out and all around, sending strength of presence up, out and throughout.

P is for...

Peace

"Peace: inner hostilities dissolved"

War and peace is a complicated beast. However, without inner peace, peace 'out there' in the world stands no chance at all.

A few days ago I heard myself saying to a neighbour, 'I like a bit of a battle'. To me though, battling isn't warring or conflict as such. Rather it's a challenge: something that contains a sense of promise of future achievement... and that must manifest very differently for everyone.

The same can be said for peace.

Conflict lies somewhere between the two. This too has many, many forms.

The important thing is to not get too caught up in any of it, whilst doing all we can to dissolve personal inner hostilities.

Here's how:

Space – full, free living space. We're talking quality, you at the centre of everything 'me' time.

Take times out.

This might be a bit weird at first. Stay with the weirdness, as this too is part of the process.

At some point you'll just get it. You won't be doing anything at all and yet you just 'get it'.

It's like a coming together with the whole of everything alive with a clarity of presence.

This beautiful experience is you getting yourself. No strings attached, just you.

What's important is, no matter the beauty of the experience, no matter the gorgeousness of the sensations... relax, letting your body live and breathe as freely as it likes, allowing it to pass as freely as it arrived.

You still have a life to live and one with its conflicts, battles, wins and losses. However, within all of that you will now have surety of presence... your youness alive and living... in your very own Oasis of Calm.

O is for...

Open

I'm sure by now you would have noticed
I use this word a lot,

'open yourself...'

This is because, complicated as we are, we acquire habitual states and ways of being to help us through the complexities of living a human life. In time these habits become unconscious and in so being relatively fixed, closed, and to varying degrees closing ourselves from the rest of life.

You've heard the phrase of wearing a number of hats, well, this alludes to some of the habits we acquire along the way. These hats we don may be for home, work, play as well as ones for different circumstances within those environments or for being with different people. All of that swapping and changing who and what we are and when – switching from one version of ourselves to another affects who and what we really are on a fundamental level - the person we know we are and feel good about being. The problem is, the more structured the hats we wear, the more we remove ourselves from our fundamental sense of self.

This process of switching creates a patterning, closing ourselves off from inherent adaptability.

Hence the need to open…

The problem with being patterned is that it affects everything: personality, character, even stops us from feeling and there is very little we can do about it. Whilst these patterned ways of being don't suit us, or maybe only suit us in the short-term, we become stuck. In time our activities, behaviours, tone, vibe and language etc. become normalised, expected even, not only by ourselves, but also by others.

Being stuck in this way also means losing freedom of movement, sensitivity and senses to our whole life experience – inside, out and throughout, affecting our whole life and life quality.

The key to stepping out of these closed, patterned ways of being is to open yourself to being your whole self. That's right, the good, the bad, the ugly and the beautiful.

Here's how:

Being closed manifests as being defensive, and the first step to becoming open once more is recognising those seemingly self-defensive behaviours, actions and interactions.

Open yourself to recognise when you have been defensive.

Obviously, there are those times when the threat is real. In these circumstances it's important to cut yourself some slack, allowing yourself to be your own best friend, ready, willing and able to stand up for yourself and stand your ground.

There will also be those other times when there is no threat at all.

Whilst the former will be understandable and the latter not, just let yourself be. This includes the aftershocks and whatever those aftershocks trigger to be whatever they are too, letting it all meander on through.

The tricky part is to not to get caught up in the whys and wherefores and especially justifications!

The act of recognising your defences are in play is enough, as it indicates things are on the move - that your personal transformation is underway, and you will be changing.

Let yourself be as gentle and self-nurturing as you like, relishing all you are and all you will be – strengthening in the space your increasing openness is revealing, loosening any fixtures, untangling the knots, breathing the lusciousness of this beautiful human quality: inherent adaptability, all around, inside, out and throughout.

And yes, all whilst allowing yourself to enjoy realising more of yourself in real life as well as those inconvenient truths as and when they arise… you'll be surprised at just how forgiving life, you and its people can be.

N is for...

Nature

"Nothing rings more true than a living
soul being free to be"

To be or not to be, that is the question – or is it?

Why not just be?

If there is one thing we shouldn't deny ourselves in life, it has to be our nature.

On a fundamental level, our nature, is what our bodies long to be, demand even. We are spawned of the planet. You see our drive 'to be' – our nature - resides deep inside, all around and throughout. There's no pinpointing it, it is just there – it just is.

Our nature is a driving force beyond all ken.

It's what makes a 'good girl' go 'off the rails' through puberty and men of all ages live to sow their oats. There's no rhyme or reason. Some urges just have to be respected for what they are – something we can't suppress. For whenever we try they will manifest elsewhere.

So, here are some things you should know:

Nature erupts during adolescence. During which time everyone is drawn to some wild, weird, wonderful, possibly dangerous things. Once things begin to settle, you will be most comfortable with your biological family. Yes, despite the differences and your struggle for independence, those natural similarities cannot be denied. We are spawned of the planet, our family and our family's families going back through the generations.

So parents, you have the most mammoth task of all – You not only have your own life to live to the full, but also to be there for your offspring – no matter what. Kudos. Stay close without suffocating; objective, loving, 'understanding' without having a clue and 'being there'... you will all be going through the best of times and the worst of time together – be in it together, simultaneously together – and apart.

Problems will arise when other factors of life: energy, environmental, economic, familial, egoistical, behavioural, social, cultural, political preferences and prejudices don't align with our nature. For example, we may be peaceable and innovative of nature, riding the storms with aplomb, yet 'lose it' completely when faced with something ridiculously trivial to those all around.

For who you really are at the most fundamental, unknowable levels to be provided freedom to be present and live as fully as possible, the key is to let yourself have your 'say' 'sway' and 'way'.

Here's how:

Of course, by now you're getting an inkling of what to do – it's back to basics!

There are two parts to this one,

Part 1 – Let go

"Your soul knows where to go for nourishing growth"

I know, it's true, and it's really tricky.

Ever since these words bubbled up from way deep within, I've had them pinned up on my work noticeboard. Despite being well aware of the truth of the words, sometimes I just can't help myself.

Sometimes, just sometimes, I do wish I knew too!

We're so human – right!

So yes, have the words to hand, especially somewhere you know you're likely to get too involved in yourself, so they are there for you as and when you need them… and yes, open to them warming the cockles of your heart, spreading lusciousness throughout whenever you catch a glimpse of them.

Our compromises in life are many and varied – most of which are also locked away in our subconscious… let go.

Part 2 - Be a nature nurturer

Get out and about in nature, as free as you like. For me this can be just stepping out the door. I immediately relax !

When we're out and about in nature, our innate symbiotic relationship with everything natural is stimulated, recharging our natural fundamentals: the organic, sensory, physiological, instinctive and intuitive. Done so with love, light and good wishes bubbling away in the background, we also enliven our inner nurturer, providing that all important breathing space for us to come to wholistic terms with those dratted compromises.

M is for...

Moments for Melting Mindsets

The human brain loves a pattern, or so they say...

Now this is fine as long as we, our mind, body, soul etc. remain loose, open with a good deal of free, full living space, as this ensures mindsets formed are purely temporary. All of which helps us, our mind, body, soul etc. remain fluid.

'Oh what a tangled web we weave...' Sir Walter Scott

... a state we can fall into through the mere act of living as best we can.

Problems arise, as always when physiological fixations are formed. In respect of mindsets, fixations arise when beliefs, theories, opinion, associations, language etc. become all-encompassing 'truths', 'facts' that neatly bring to peace a mish–mash of misperceptions. Such mindsets provide a sense of self that falls short of the person's whole, full and potential self.

As far as our brain, mind, senses and intelligences are concerned, this means we close the circle. We complete ourselves and in so doing close ourselves off from everything outside of those circles.

Further problems arise due to reality generated by mindsets: the gaps between these and reality, and how those gaps are filled. Whilst there is, of course, a limit to which we can effectively fill those gaps, our ability to do so is enormous. To further complicate matters, as is our way, these fillers take many forms: we make up sense that is on the whole, nonsense. We blame, justify, punish, submit, give up, fight and seek revenge.

In fact we do almost anything to return to a sense of peace, completion, wholeness – peace of mind, body, spirit and soul – albeit temporary.

Even more problems arise through having to negotiate and navigate everyone else's fillers... as well as our own.

Hence the need for a good dose of Moments for Melting Mindsets, all round.

Yes, the brain takes on an enormous amount of strain.

The beauty of Moments for Melting Mindsets, is that it gives the whole of you a chance to let everything slip away to free up that all important free, full living space – inside, out and throughout… leaving all the good stuff of your brain, mind, senses and intelligences to be a little more freely whilst reconnecting, recharging and living clearer and brighter.

Here's how:

Sleep is essential, and I'm talking good quality, well ready for a good night's sleep, sleep is the way to go.

As and when this isn't happening for you, take a break and have a rest – WHEN YOU DON'T NEED TO

Take time out to let everything go whilst grounding, centring, breathing freely and fully as you possibly can.

Invite your brain to rest, melting away and relaxing your whole nervous system all the way to the tip of your coccyx, its lusciousness spreading throughout.

Sighing, stretching, moving, swaying, let its vitality flow.

"No Pressure"

This getting your whole self on board can be helped along with brain melting activities dotted throughout the day. Such as loving, silence, immersion in nature. It's all about doing things that make you feel whole, like yourself: come alive, whilst being peaceful, rested and relaxed, sprinkled with a good dose of vitality.

Not forgetting those magical qualities of life: birdsong, free joyous laughter, things of natural beauty.

Letting all these things be…

Fully enjoying those precious moments of free, full connectivity with the lusciousness of life they bring – inside, out and throughout.

Being with…

L is for...

Light

Light just is.

Light does not move, yet it is far from static.

Light is life and life is light.

Light is warmth, warming all it touches.

Light can be direct, deflected and reflected...always illuminating, lighting paths.

Light's presence brings varying degrees of darkness. However,

"Even in the darkest of darks...

where there's life, there's light..."

Let yours shine!

Here's how:

Let your light shine through. Yes, even when it's at its faintest, when you are your most dark, your light still shines – somewhere.

It may seem all life has been snuffed out, but it remains in the deepest darkest recesses, it's there, all aglow.

Let it be, let it glow, let go and let it grow.

Light is clearing, and of course light ha!

Light feels good.

The more you let go, loosen, open, untangle, the freer its pathways.

The more freely light circulates, the more it touches, the more it warms....

... the lighter, shinier, brighter and clearer you become

K is for...

Kuchisabishii...

... a uniquely Japanese expression for lonely mouth.

I happened upon this word and immediately connected with what it describes.

A lonely mouth

Our mouths mark our first connection with physical sustenance from outside of ourselves.

Quite bizarrely, I experienced the sensation of a lonely mouth this week. It was getting late in the evening and I had a fancy for something. I could tell the pull wasn't from my gut – I wasn't hungry as such, but I needed something.

Some describe kuchisabishii as mindless eating, but for me it goes much deeper. For me, kuchsabishii describes a longing for... and a longing for what cannot be satisfied through food... or anything else for that matter.

Kuchsabishii describes an inner emptiness that is longing to be filled - with being alive and living.

It all stems from our first feed and the fundamentally powerful experience it is. Our first feed is also our first experience of satisfaction, contentment, fullness, one that is a natural, relatively freely available source of sustenance and so much more. The feeding experience also sparks the connection between 2 lives: the one providing nutrition and the one receiving it, their relationship, future life and living experiences.

Kuchisabishii in adulthood signals something missing - a disconnection from ourselves. Through that disconnection, the mouth longs for something, but we can't know what, so we fill the void with something, possibly through something that's satisfied before. Should this prove fruitful we experience the sweet taste of success. However, if and when it falls short, we are left lacking.

So yes, a lonely mouth, kuchisabishii goes way beyond the mouth, food and nutrition. Kuchisabishii stems from our disconnections manifesting as physiological needs.

Something to 'stay with' awhile.

Here's how:

As freely as you like, being grounded, centred, alive and living whilst melting your brain and freeing yourself of attachment, open yourself to all the good stuff of life, inside, out and throughout.

Gently letting go of everything that makes you less than whole, inviting in everything nourishing.

Allowing your light free passage, freeing and strengthening your connections to everything that brings you alive to thrive.

Whilst you're there, allow your mind to have a wander... your body breathing in around and throughout everything that makes you you – that endures no matter what and is nourishing, strengthening and empowering.

Beginning to open to appreciate everything you are and everything you have, because that is all of you and your life right now.

This is your starting point: your ground zero.

Your body breathing it all around, breathing life into all the parts other breaths have yet to reach, feeling that sense of appreciation, fullness, satisfaction, contentment, and yes, even happiness.

Stay with awhile allowing bubbles of renewal, health, wealth and happiness to spread...

... for a smile to form.

You have so got this.

J is for...

JJ

Joy

O M Goodness, Joy is such a beautiful thing... but what is it?

I was a little surprised when I searched for a definition of joy.

I certainly know the experience, sensation and feelings, but as to the science, I have no clue. The best starting point when I don't know something I'm curious about is to begin with a definition of the word. However, in this case, it was a stopping point.

Fair enough, the definition of the noun, 'joy' is, 'the sign of great pleasure and happiness'. It was the contextual use of the verb, 'to rejoice' that caused my consternation:

> 'I felt shame that I had ever joyed in his discomfiture or pain'

To me it seemed bizarre to marry such a sensation of pleasure with one of discomfort – joy and shame...

So I asked some friends...

... and things began to fall into place...

Joy in itself is enough!

Whilst it is different for different people, joy in itself is enough - a gorgeous thing. It is a phenomenal phenomenon of human beingness. And isn't it amazing - wonderfully joyous even, that we do get to be joyous.

Joy is gorgeous aspect of human beingness, and when alive and living freely in people, and it gets to bubble up and out into the wider world, it is contagious.

No matter what, joy is joyous, and when free to be and free to spread whenever and wherever, all the better.

So what of the contextual definition of earlier – what's that all about?

Ah yes, those simultaneous and mixed feelings that come from living patterns – an wholistic incoherence. Whereas, wholistic joy marks a vitality of vibrations that run throughout touching, enlivening every aspect of our being, inside, out, throughout and out beyond ourselves, living patterns stymie that flow giving rise to conflict.

The good news is, life-limiting living patterns that give rise to these conflicts can be dispersed - with the help of joy.

Life is so much easier when sprinkled with joy. It's like joy and shared joy marks a freedom of being that we should all enjoy at some point or other through our day. Joy is a state of open and free yet full unconditionality – a celebration that shows we are indeed alive, living and up for everything our lives have to offer - yes, the highs, lows and everything in between.

As far as joy is concerned, the starting point is satisfaction. As Maslow identified way back when, without that inner sense of wholeness brought about by satisfaction, life is indeed limited to satisfying those needs. However, once satisfaction is realised wholistically, it leads to happiness and joy overflowing to abundance.

"nothing

rings

more

true

than

a

living

soul

that's

free

to

be"

Here's how:

Let yourself go and open yourself to abundance – yours, your life's and life's abundance inside, out and throughout.

Give yourself permission to reacquaint yourself with all the good stuff of your life – inside, out and throughout.

Open yourself to everything that is precious to you – yes, even those things of your subconscious.

Allow space and time for things to begin to move, letting your whole self be.

Once that realisation of satisfaction hits home, let it spread throughout as gently as you like – things have shifted…

All the while living and breathing in all the more free, full space, allowing all things precious to gain strength of being through you.

Open yourself to pleasure – one of our most overlooked, more internal senses, allowing time and space for those experiences of pleasure to spread throughout.

After a while you should begin to experience bubbles of joy popping inside.

Whilst this can be a bit weird, just let everything – all you are, all you have ever been and all you will ever be – be, allowing those sensations of joyous, luscious gorgeousness spread throughout...

... a wholly complete smile forming in its own good time...

... bliss.

I is for...

Ideas

Ideas stem from the progressive side of
our spirit, up and through the more abstract parts of our brain to emerge from having travelled through the creative aspects of our minds.

Exploring the world is innate. All living creatures must eat and growing, hunting, gathering is part of our fundamental makeup. We are, in essence explorers. Add to this a spirit of adventure and that exploration becomes one filled with ideas around resourcefulness and communication… of course, when given free, full living space to be so.

I know this well, for this has been me in many different guises. A few weeks ago, I realised yet another dismantling of one of these old guises – an internal self-built mechanism that had formed through the mere act of me living my life. Yes, a mechanism and patterns that generated ideas out of necessity rather than just being alive and living.

"Letting go of everything I became to survive"

Yes, I'd been through some scrapes in my time.

The realisation began as a pounding in my temples, no doubt that was the part of my brain from where all those ideas had popped. A few days later, and I began to have thoughts, unnecessary thoughts – yes, I actually felt the un-necessity of them. In fact, I felt they were getting in the way of me living my life. I let them be. Words, just words, and yes, words had been my bread and butter for a long time. Letting them be with a good dose of nurturing in tow. However, this turned into a realisation of the generator itself – right in my gut… churning away. I had no choice, but to get up and begin to write – this. The pounding in my temples is…

… and so I left things there and prepared to go out for a walk. I had banged up my foot pretty badly the other week – an old war wound playing up. This would be my first time out after that in proper boots.

Grounding and centring soundly with Reiki, tensions began to ease sufficient to get me up and moving.

Time in Nature is my best form of therapy, and this time was no different. Clearing that all important living space inside, out and throughout – an aura cleanse extraordinaire.

The pounding remained, and took some time to dissipate.

The mechanism was one of old and generated out of necessity – seeming and otherwise.

As I said when returning from the walk,

'new ways need space'

The old are doing just that, generating space in their dissipation – it just takes a little time with lots of care and attention.

"the old ways are crumbling – let it"

All these unnecessary tensions that have built up over time tie up our imagination, intuition, instincts, senses, intelligences, communications as well as our activities, affecting everything we are. That is, everything we are, everything we bring into life and everything life becomes.

Letting be, letting go, sending them on their way is the only way out of the deadly embraces these ingrained tensions form.

"New ways need free, full living space,

old ways are crumbling – let it"

Here's how:

Central to dissipating unnecessaries is some form of safe, well-grounded and centred free living with the space for free expression and movement.

Open yourself to any such opportunities, breathe in, around and all about – enjoying to the full the sense of joy that emerges with ideas, letting whatever comes of them to come to life in its own good time... it will.

H is for...

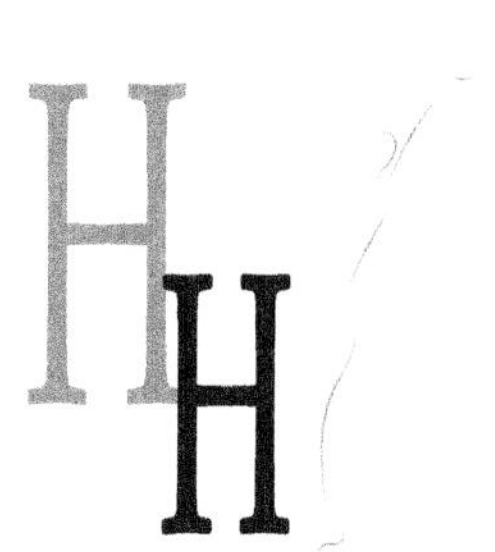

Herd

The human herd is an extraordinary beast.

Each person unique in their own right, sharing a myriad of qualities with any number of others, yet remaining separate and distinctive. Those others are not limited to other humans either, for we also share many characteristics and qualities with all other forms of life. There can be no doubt though, a human is a human is a human, and you are you – the one and only you.

Like birds we flock together, building relationships, collecting in tribes through mutual connections, interests, activities, predispositions, predilections, qualities and environments, and yet. Yes, we remain wholly connected with, present in and active participants in the whole of life as part of the whole human herd – past, present and future.

And that, my dear friends can be a tricky thing to get your head around sufficiently for the rest of you to become reacquainted and live well with – wholistically.

Yes, who and what you are, I am, we are today affects everything we are and everything we become - our future as well as the future of life on this fair planet of ours – our home.

For the most part there is very little we can do to change the run of things, for, just as we are each a culmination of everything that's ever happened, so too is life. However, we can become better placed in ourselves with the whole of everything and everyone else by letting go of anything that keeps us apart – any forced or exaggerated and unnecessary distinctions and similarities.

Here's how:

Have a wander around the ideas put forward, remaining unique with a whole unique life of your own to live with the whole of humanity – past, present and future… allowing it all to settle in your own good time.

Allowing all your underlying connections to open, becoming free moving channels, alive and living - buzzing, if you like, like electricity running throughout. Feels good doesn't it - just to be alive and living in the whole of everything – enjoy!

Things may need shifting around, just be open to being your best – good for yourself, everyone and everything else for that matter – and take your time, giving yourself all the time, space and resources you need, making yours the most pleasant, lightest and easiest path possible.

Yes, let go, breathing all that good stuff of life, humanity and yourself in, around and throughout…

We are all so worth it.

"new

ways

of

being

and

living

need

free,

full

living

space"

G is for...

Generations... and their Gaps

This is a biggie - and it has again been tricky for me to write, as I was letting go generational effects!

We are each affected by the generation factor, coloured by the time in human history in which we spend our formative years. There's nothing we can do about this phenomenon of our existence, growth and development process. However, we can ensure no edges form, as these are the stuff of generation gap formation, disconnection etc. etc.. This can prove problematic, as we do have a tendency of wrapping things of life into nice, neat little packages, tying them up with strings and filing them away...

For example, most recently, the term 'Geriatric Millennial', has been coined to describe those Generation Ys born in the early eighties, as they spent their formative years in amongst a pivotal shift in our technology from analogue to digital. Rather than it being what it is – an aha! for those born within that time frame - one of their multitude of personal markers, it has become a potential edge in the workplace. A potential edge in the workplace that can set these people apart not only from everyone else, but, has the real possibility of setting them apart from themselves.

A word to the wise from someone who cut her teeth in big industry in amongst the shift from manual systems and processes to digital, when efficiency, effectiveness and economy had become the new religion fuelling the capitalist 80s... whatever all that was defined me as an employee, a potential employee and as the person I became. It defined me inside, out and throughout. However, throughout that whole amazingly successful and pleasurable whirl of living on the edge, whatever I was wasn't the real me. I 'had it all', and yet there was always something missing.

Whilst throughout I'd denied myself as a person of religion, I'd unknowingly become indoctrinated by the religion of industrial efficiency, effectiveness and economy... a 'professionalism' that coloured my whole life.

So, as I said before, we are each born into one or other time – a generation of human life on this planet, and yes, those things do influence what we become.

What's important is to recognise these factors as single facets amongst our multitude.

Now, this would not be a problem if we were in some way able to remain connected to, and alive and living in and with the whole of everything. However, this is far from the case… we all do what we can, when we can, wherever we can - we live first!

To further exacerbate this macro-generational effect, we have the family and group dynamic generational effects too. Again, due to their purely circumstantial nature, development is seemingly seamless – natural even. However, because of the inherent limitations of both family and any groups we subsequently become part of, as well as our drive to be ourselves anyway, our development becomes stymied.

In our drive to be ourselves anyway, we aspire to be some people, are inspired by others, avoid some, resist others and secure comradery with many. All the time this is happening, we're acquiring patterns for living, navigation and negotiation that, unbeknownst to ourselves are only relevant at the point in time in which they are lived. However, because these activities define what we become and vice versa, in time we become patterned in our ways of living. The more embedded the patterns, the more difficult is ongoing growth, development etc., especially in respect of living through change.

Whilst all of these factors progress our lives, they can also cut us off from who and what we actually are – our innate selves, skills, talents, abilities, art, personality and character.

All told, all generational effects mark steps of progression in our human life map. However, without a vitality of connection with, and appreciation of the whole of human history, generation gaps will remain too tight for real wholistic progression to be made.

The good news is no matter what year, decade, generation, family or culture any of us are born into, on some level we remain connected to the whole of everything, who and what we are and what floats our boat.

Yes, there will always be generational benefits and detriments, what's important is to not capitalise on either, as you can be compromising yourself. As long as our underlying intention is to be ourselves in a healthy, happy, fulfilling and sustainable way, we won't stray too far from being so.

Covid-19 is a significant marker in contemporary human history, because it is one we have all experienced. That's right, every single one of us has been affected by it. In this respect it did bring us together as one life form on this planet susceptible to another - a significant other that marked a significant difference beyond all the petty differences that keep us humans apart from each other.

As we step forward into another moment, hour, day. year, time of human existence, having all been affected by this pandemic, we each have the opportunity to be part of a stronger human presence - to be more of ourselves and more with the whole of humanity.

Each and every one of us has something unique to add to the rich tapestry that is life. Being yourself, and yes, on some level 'knowing' you are being yourself and doing everything that makes you come alive is exactly what makes the picture come to life – and beautifully.

"everything

we

are

affects

everything

we

are"

Here's how:

You becoming what you are right now began way back in the mists of time itself. Yes, way beyond anything generational, all boundaries and anything else for that matter.

Soak that up for a moment – maybe breathing it in, all around and throughout and having a sleep on it all... after all, it's a big thing isn't it.

Whenever possible, give yourself a break – from anything and everything that gives you hassle, whilst building in some strong, yet flexible and adaptable cushioning. Remind yourself of what it feels like for you to be at home in your own skin, in life with the whole of humanity, everything that's important to you, everything that makes you satisfied, happy, alive and living.

Wherever possible, letting all your loving gorgeousness flow throughout.

Breathing it all in, around and throughout – your uniqueness, the incredibility of you being here at all at this point in time of our existence, everything you have ever been, all you are to be, your joys… allowing that sense of groundedness to settle you here on this planet, bubbling with life, being alive and living – and enjoying the experience, letting everything else go.

Now, when you have a moment, take time out to settle into the whole world of people, past present and future, allowing space, time even, if possible, for them to do likewise. We each have something to offer the space we find ourselves in, which is great in concept, not so easily defined in reality. We are each, at times, too demanding of each other. Clashes are inevitable – and potentially painful. The best thing to do when a clash arises is to excuse yourself, securing distance between, space and time away.

Whilst 'away', allow yourself to be just what you are, grounding, centring and breathing as best you can, calming, settling and letting your joy arise. Then as quietly and gently as you please allow your whole self to get on board with the situation – for real, always open to the fact that for every person or experience that gives you hassle, there will be any number of others that will be nourishing.

Sometimes these clashes will arise from nowhere as a completely new experience, other times there will be clashes of old in new circumstances. Take your time, allowing your own whole sense to come to the fore in its own good time.

Sometimes this will be via your intuitive, instinctive, rational, irrational, other times emotional, maybe philosophical, sometimes even ridiculous, just let your senses and sense making be whatever it is, as and when it is.

The more you practice the letting yourself be, coming home, settling and becoming happy in your own self, the easier things will become.

Whilst all of that more internal stuff is happening, open yourself to gravitate without preference nor prejudice towards people, activities and experiences that are nourishing, lighting, enlightening and clearing your way – on all counts - they will be many, varied and yes, of all ages.

F is for...

Fright, Fight, Flight

I have a bit of a love affair... with the human body.

Such an amazing bit of kit – so wondrously complicated and yet, so simply beautiful. You can tell, can't you – yes, I am just a tad enamoured with it all... and despite its inherent challenges of which we all have many.

So what's that got to do with fright, fight, flight...?

My stress-busting nemesis and ***the*** major confounder of all wholistic progress in our lives is our fright, flight, fight mechanism - the necessary, yet super-entangling Sympathetic Nervous System.

It is absolutely necessary, as it stimulates heightened awareness, and super-entangling, as it is involuntary...

So you can imagine can't you the first time that heightened awareness hits home, and just how not prepared we are to make full and proper sense of it all – it's a bugger!

The ensuing emotional, spiritual, rational, behavioural, activity and energy entanglements lead to all sorts of trouble from intellectualisation, drama, sensationalisms and panics of all sorts to real dramas – conflicts, anxieties, stresses and fears.

The only way out of the entanglements our nervous system causes is through untangling.

Here's how:

Remember your Oasis of Calm? This is where it comes into the fore.

The aim is to settle, calm and relax, melting your brain, enabling your whole nervous system to get on board with the whole of you in the whole of your life and life – past, present and future.

Allow the sense of this to sink in, gaining a deeper appreciation, awareness even for everything.

As it all flows through, breathe it in, around and throughout, enjoying the sensations of you being alive, living safe and sound – everything ticking over just nicely.

Let go of everything you have ever been, whilst immersing yourself in everything you are, everything you have going for you and all you are to be. Breathing nice and slow, loosening as you go, deepening your flow, awakening to the idea of your heightened awareness, fright, fight, flight and letting all be just what it is.

Safe and sound, all around with that sense of spark, lightness and glow, being fully alive and living in your life to come.

Letting go a little more, open your senses to the planet, experiencing your natural connection to this and everything else.

Breathing a little calmer, deeper, loosening some more, opening yourself to your whole life happening in, throughout and out through you - living it to the full – the challenges, heartaches, good times and bad.

Living is so much easier, and simpler with your whole self on board.

The more you practice, the more it becomes second nature.

"your

potential

is for you

to grow

into,

hang on

in

there…

it may

be a

bumpy

ride"

E is for...

Education

Education, just what is it?

I can remember asking myself, way back when – 'why do we go to school?' It seemed a reasonable question, about which everyone had their own opinion. None of which fits what I've learnt from people's experiences of it.

Here are some examples, "I hated it." This came to light when secondary school years were coloured grey on a client's life map – "I just want to blot it all out, for it to not be there." This was an extreme case, as on that level, not only were they blotting out their experience of secondary education, but also a whole five years of formative life experience, in school and elsewhere. Others, somewhat at the other extreme, declared a love for theirs, almost with a yearning to go back, confirming the myth, as "the best years of my life." Of course there were many, many other variations between. Overall though, each and every one focussed primarily on either positive or negative personal experience on the pleasure/pain spectrum.

As to what it did for people, what they actually got out of it, I am still no clearer.

And that is, in part, what has stimulated this little piece… Here we have my take on what education should be.

"education:

spark

knowledge

understanding

consideration

application

experience

time & space

assessment

exploration

synergy"

See that potential up there in the quote on page 88? Well my take on what education should be revolves around allowing the person to do just that – grow into their potential… whilst smoothing the ride.

And that, my friends is all about the individual flourishing.

I happened across some steps in the education process – the mechanics if you like, which I have since expanded upon. Whilst this might seem too mechanical to the more abstract among us, once seen wholistically, can help smooth the way.

Spark – we all know what that is right – it's inspirational, clearing, triggering a green light all the way inside and out. It's a,

Woohoo! Yes I can! Positivity! Optimism!

A 'good to be aliveness'.

In whichever way that expresses itself through you, the senses this positivity triggers are ones of openness to adventure, curiosity, exploration, aliveness - up for it.

Knowledge – everything that's ever been experienced before translating itself into facts. The tricky thing about knowledge is discerning between facts and theory, theory and knowledge, knowledge and beliefs, beliefs and myths. Much of what we learn in education is purported to be fact when, in fact it's not. Furthermore, much of what is known outside of education doesn't get communicated. As long as we can hang loose, freeing our brain, body, intelligence and senses etc., all should be well-ish.

Understanding – is comprehension of a communication from one person, thing or other. Understanding is easily recognised as the nodding of the head, which may only happen after a little further exploration. In this respect, understanding is another positive experience, this time of a message being communicated, received and understood. The penny drops. With a fair wind and looseness around knowledge, it should remain that way – that ability to understand, not understand and all points between interspersed throughout your mind.

Consideration – sparks, knowledge and understanding are best served with a good helping of consideration. Consideration is a neurological process, which we don't have to do as such, as the brain, when allowed to be so, is a super processor of all this stuff. Our brain, happily ensconced in the whole of ourselves is built for cogitating, reviewing, retrieving, assessing and finessing to form potential knowledge.

Application – is activity, doing, living. Every moment of every day we become something different to the last - we're alive, we live, we're active, we are interactive, we take stuff on board, lose other stuff, grow, develop, we get stuff done, we affect things and in so doing, we experience.

Experience – lived experience is the consequential effect of everything that's ever been lived before. It is the effect on ourselves of simultaneous living, growing, developing, becoming and being. As our aim in life is to flourish, any knocks along the way have to be fully lived, healed, recovered from, all whilst doing everything else – extraordinarily difficult and time consuming, so much so we can become entangled in an experiential loop.

Time and space – The only way to grow through experience is with a good helping of time and space. Experience plus time and space provides opportunity to finesse, yielding self-knowledge. That is, that depth of knowledge that confirms all the stuff of you and all you just 'know': everything that makes you come alive, shine and thrive for life.

Assessment – is a process of mulling and a culling – sorting the wheat from the chaff that can only be done well through times out. When I say, times out, I mean proper times out from everything other than yourself, everything you are and everything that aids your flourishing. Sleep is essential, good, wholesome sleeps is central to the education process.

Exploration – assessment may well lead to further exploration that's different to the one of the spark, this one is more intelligent based. Intelligent exploration is research. The more open minded the research, the better. Again without proper time out this can lead to another entangled cycle of research and assessment without any actual progress, growth or development. Space between the two is once again essential.

And now back to the good news in the education process…

Synergy – Oh what joy – when things come together inside, out and throughout that speeds you on your way. Synergy marks the 'dropped penny' from 'understanding' having done its full rounds becoming an wholistic 'A-ha!' that can be euphoric. Enjoy these smoothing, lifting, enlivening path clearers – to the full and wholistically. They are indeed the stuff of our connectivity to everyone and everything that mark those all so precious moments when we are indeed one, yet progressing alone.

So yes, as you can see, there is rather a lot to this thing we call education, isn't there – a complicated little beast that all becomes a bit of a muddle without proper space and time out.

No one thing should be blotted out of your life, because the fact of the matter is that it can't. You are you right now, because of every moment you have ever lived – the good, the bad, the downright ugly and beautiful. That said, any blots on your travels along the way need, and take time to heal. Allow yourself that time.

Here's how:

Rest without having to have one!

For the super-active among us this can be truly tricky, but once you break the cycle and take charge, communicating loud and clear to yourself that your life is of paramount importance, there will be no stopping you.

Let go, shedding any debris, letting it fall away into the mists of time.

Breathing nice and slow, fully in your flow, letting your body move as you go

Turn your attention ever so gently to your essence – the essence of everything you are, deep in your core.

You are life primed to shine and thrive in all you are and all you do.

Who are you...?

What are all the good things people say about you...?

What floats your boat...?

You know what I mean, all the stuff you do that makes you come alive, be yourself and feel like you are being yourself and living your life to the full.

When your mind wanders, what life do you dream of for yourself?

If you were to be granted 3 wishes, what would they be...?

What are your secrets...?

What hidden talents do you long to explore...?

Open yourself to live your very best version of yourself.

Clearing, lightening and brightening in gentle acknowledgement of your life here, right now.

Your life gaining strength of presence, spreading throughout, out beyond your senses, breathing life into everything you are.

D is for...

Disruption

Disruption is a fact of life that's woven into the very fabric of existence.

Whilst peace, love, light, togetherness, abundance and understanding form gorgeous aspects of life, there's no getting away from the fact that disruptions are happening all the time.

"Eruptions, shifts, triggering something else, chain reactions, the final straws, tipping points, something's got to give – life is one of constant disruption"

There's the universal, planetary, inter-species and yes, even intra-species. So, there's no small wonder we all live in some form of conflict – inside, out and throughout.

The tricky bit is that we humans are pretty good at smoothing that conflict – so much so, we submit: become placid, complacent, comfortable, which, whilst a form of living, isn't alive and living. One of the bedfellows of this forced passivity is, of course stress.

Trickier still is when stepping out of that passivity.

Oh yes, all change, planned and otherwise can be stressful... unless...

The key to stepping out anyway, and giving your chance of living a full and happy life a good go, is acceptance and to be accepting of everything…

"peace:

inner

hostilities

dissolved"

Here's how:

You want to be you, a happy you - alive and living your life to the full. Allow the words to sink in, float all around, inside and throughout,

"I want to be me, a happy me –

alive and living my life to the full."

Breathe in its vitality, beyond the words to your senses and sensations around them. Allowing its freeing yet fulfilling energy to travel freely all around, inside and out - enlivening your whole self, body and soul.

As we have seen, there will be conflict, this is inevitable – life is full of it.

Disruption is inevitable

Take times out – alive and living time outs, getting your whole self on board with the reality of living a human life – your life.

Taking wholistic 'me' times wherever and whenever you can.

Especially when things are going well.

Not to collapse into mind, rather to enliven and strengthen all you are and everything you are about - to emerge, shinier, livelier and thrivier.

Relaxing into your Oasis of Calm when disruptions arise.

Then there are those times of inner conflict. Begin to open yourself to be aware of all the times you stop yourself from being free to be yourself. Times like these are fuelled with conflict.

Be free to be yourself – no matter what.

This is your life and this is your chance to shine and thrive; to be abundant in all you are.

There is no doubt, it will be tough at times, but my goodness, the payoffs will be more than worth it.

We only have one shot at life - let's make it a good one !

C is for...

Core

Inner resources have a good name, they
are seen as a good thing and applauded. However, it is a little known fact that a stressful or challenging life can build inner resources that are unsustainable.

'... what doesn't kill you makes you stronger!'

has its limitations.

What we're not told is those inner resources, resolve, resilience etc. can also disconnect us from ourselves, life and everything in it, stymying growth, development and personal progress. Constrained in this way, from the inside out, the person also contracts away from life, and continues to do so on a self-limiting cycle – again, from the inside out.

Free the core!

Yes, freeing the core is the key to liberating the whole – your youness, body, heart, mind, spirit and soul.

Here's how:

The core is your essence that resides throughout. However, it can be most felt, experienced through engaging, enlivening and aligning the Chakra. Each Chakra provides a different flavour – its own unique signature that adds its own ingredient to the recipe that is the whole of your essence.

The main Chakra are:

Crown - providing senses of clarity;

Third Eye - insight, foresight and intelligence;

Throat - presence, voice and identity;

Heart - of course, love;

Solar Plexus – satisfaction, appreciation, drive and joy;

Sacral - nurturing, sexuality and the

Base - Nature and your Nature

Combined, they make for the truly amazing phenomenon that is the stuff of vitality: all the stuff of being alive and living; a vitality that is at its best when free flowing.

Let the words resonate throughout whilst breathing life in, around and throughout.

Very often just a gentle acknowledgement of having such a beautiful aspect such as an essence is sufficient to begin untangling, loosening, relaxing and clearing any areas of pressure, tension, stress or fear.

Whilst doing so, allow your vitality to sparkle into life, spreading throughout, remaining as loose and free to your life's possibilities as is possible.

It's very easy to get caught up in thoughts and feelings. Wherever possible let them be just what they are, spreading throughout without getting caught up anywhere along their way.

Sometimes, we can do nought else but get caught up in them and that's okay too. The worst possible thing is to get yourself in a tangle of beating yourself up.

Even so, should this happen, yes, you're getting to know the drill, let this be just what it is too.

No matter what, treat yourself with kindness, be gentle, as those more kindly juices ease the flow, strengthening all you are, your potential and all you will be as you go.

As and when allow yourself to enjoy being alive and living.

No fanfare, just the slightest of acknowledgements with a gentle nod to the wise, allowing a soft smile to form from deep within.

You are your all.

Namaste

B is for...

Beauty

Beauty is edgeless symmetry that dwells
momentarily in the beholder. It is in those oh so special moments that we too are living in a state of edgeless symmetry; our innate beauty is alive and living.

We respond in many ways when confronted with life's beauties. Like everything pleasantly surprising, they pop up out of nowhere when we least expect it, making them extraordinarily difficult to live wholistically.

It's akin to fright, fight, flight - only pleasant.

Whilst this state of beauty is a temporary and fleeting gorgeousness, it's a good one to experience.

It is a warm, lush, sparkly pleasure that sends nourishing vibes throughout. Helping to send those stressy ones on their way, whilst providing rest, healing, recovery, renewal and strengthening throughout.

Be aware, this state of beauty, like anything else pleasurable can lead to craving, a searching for, a hunting down, following, finding or chasing. As soon as we slip into any of those modes we become edgy.

Beauty is precious indeed; a freedom from disruption and stress in a life of abundance.

Live it well.

It takes space and lots of it to let it be, and in so being, experience it, let it live throughout, be stronger for it and be yours well.

Here's how:

What is important to note is beauty's nourishing factor. Just as you wouldn't want to rush anything of any depth of pleasure, these moments of beauty are to be savoured.

Allow yourself to take in these words and, when all's well, signal yourself to be, enjoy and be abundant in all the gorgeousness you are.

A is for…

Authenticity

It is a big word isn't it – by that I mean,
loaded with meaning, but what is it? What is authenticity?

We 'know' when we witness authenticity, primarily because we recognise inauthenticity. Even then, sorting the wheat from the chaff is incredibly difficult.

Indeed, who amongst us has never been duped?

The problem is, once duped, trust is knocked out of shape.

In many ways all we need to be aware of is that we have innate authenticity and inauthenticity detectors, senses for it, antennae if you like.

Loosening, whilst strengthening our senses and intelligences sharpens their acuity.

Now, what of our own authenticity?

What does it mean when we are being our authentic selves? What does it feel like? What of the experience – for others as well as ourselves?

It's all about being yourself, feeling as though you are being yourself, progressing through life just as you would wish to – feeling good and feeling good about yourself.

Now, whatever that is for you is yours and yours alone. It's impossible to identify, pinpoint and attach labels to - you just 'know' and that is all there is to it.

Here's how:

Let your entanglements formed of mistrust - busyness, noise, over-reaction, drama, knee-jerk responses, politics, intellectualisations, beliefs etc. reveal themselves, enjoying all.

That may sound a little odd. However, you are all those things and a little bit of humour around your limitations adds space and fluidity, aiding the healing process. Relaxing to your core, breathing it all in, around and throughout, opening yourself to freeing yourself from entanglements: past, present and future.

We are highly intelligent beings, adapting to ever-changing situations at the drop of a hat – all of which can take its toll. Whilst our intelligence is built to sort our wheat from the chaff, much of which is done behind the scenes, we can become too heavily dependent on its more cognitive aspects.

To break its hold we turn to the quantum aspects of life where life is beyond all rhyme, reason… Relaxing your brain and breathing space throughout, open yourself to the vitality in each and every one of your cells. A universe in miniature, each and every cell of every living creature playing its part in the great symphony that is life – your life.

Let go, immersing yourself into the whole of everything, loosening entanglements and breathing life in, around and throughout and into your organic filtering processes: your intelligences.

Take your time, we have to live and experience to grow and develop. Much of our progress happens beyond our cognitive powers. Allowing our innate intelligences to be free aids our free, yet fully present flow with whatever arises, moves, shifts, confronts, distracts and antagonises.

Opening, loosening and relaxing your senses, begin to enjoy being yourself: an intelligent, sentient, alive and living human being with a wholly unique and precious life to live.

As you travel along, allow 'pennies to drop' into place, delivering senses of clarity, A-has! Breathe their gorgeousness all around and throughout, opening your feet to the ground and your senses to everything all around, inside and out – your world has just expanded – enjoy! Let loose, shaking out any lingering debris. Fully strengthening everything you are from the ground up, inside out, allowing a soft smile to form.

You have so got this... x

"healing

is

all

about

taking

charge

of

yourself,

your life,

all you are

and

all you do

-

naturally"

MORE ABOUT THE AUTHOR

Like most, Pat just keeps on living through the toughest of times…. We live first – right ! In retrospect though, Pat's last two decades were beyond tough, triggered by the death of her beautiful sister, Veronica at way too young an age in 2005, compounded by menopause and caring. Even Pat's inbuilt working class resilience crumbled away, leaving her to rebuild from scratch and sometimes from the darkest of dark places.

What had been her strong affinity with life, nature, people, living well and clearing life's pathways was torn apart, sending her spiralling deep down inside, realising fragmentation galore. However, it was the essence of, 'all those things that endured no matter what' that played a pivotal role in getting her through to emerge anew. And so the paths she clears now are inside, out and throughout – not just for this moment, or for today - for life!

A caring, sharing, nurturing soul with an acuity of mind and a somewhat mischievous spirit, Pat puts you, your life and your future centre stage in her therapies and this, her first piece of writing with love, light and good wishes in the hope it helps you too emerge into your healthier, happier, shinier, livelier and thrivier future.

You, life and everything is soooo much more than we can possibly imagine…

Printed in Great Britain
by Amazon